British Library Cataloguing in Publication Data

Hately, David
    The Christmas story
    1. Jesus Christ, Childhood
    I. Title   II. Breeze, Lynn   III. Series
    232.9'2
    ISBN 0-7214-1190-8

First edition

Published by Ladybird Books Ltd Loughborough Leicestershire UK
Ladybird Books Inc Auburn Maine 04210 USA
Printed in England

The Christmas Story

written by David Hately
illustrated by Lynn Breeze

Ladybird Books

In a small town called Nazareth there lived a girl whose name was Mary.

The house she lived in had a flat roof, with stone steps leading up to it. Sometimes Mary would climb up to the roof and look down at the children playing. Mary loved children.

When Mary was old enough to marry, she was betrothed to a good man called Joseph. He was a carpenter.

One day, as Mary was busy at home, the room filled with a bright light.

An angel stood before her, and he said, "Hail, Mary! You are full of grace! The Lord is with you!"

Mary was trembling. But the angel said, "Do not be afraid. God wants to send you a baby son. When he is born, you are to call him Jesus."

And Mary smiled. "If that is what God wants, then I am happy," she said.

Now the Emperor commanded that all the men in the land should go to the town where they had been born.

There they had to sign a special book so that the Emperor would know how many people lived in this part of his empire.

Joseph had been born in a little town called Bethlehem. It was a long way from Nazareth. He had to walk all the way. Mary went, too, riding beside her husband on a donkey.

Mary was very tired when at last
they arrived in Bethlehem.

She knew that it was nearly time
for her baby to be born. She hoped
that they could find a place to rest.

But everywhere was full. There was
no room in any of the inns.

At the last place they tried, the
innkeeper saw how tired Mary
looked.

"I've no room to spare in my
inn," he said. "But, if you like,
you can stay in the stable."

Mary and Joseph thanked him.
A stable was better than nothing.

The stable was warm and quiet, and there was plenty of clean straw.

Mary and Joseph had to share it with some oxen. The animals stared curiously, and watched the little donkey eating their hay for its supper.

Joseph unpacked the food and clothes they had brought. Then he made a soft bed of straw for Mary to lie on.

That night, Mary's baby was born.

It was a boy, and they named him Jesus, just as the angel had said they must.

Mary wrapped the Baby Jesus in warm shawls. There was no cot for him to lie in, but there was a manger.

The manger was a little wooden box. The innkeeper kept it filled with hay for his animals to eat.

So Joseph put some fresh straw in the manger to make a soft bed for the Baby Jesus.

In the fields nearby, some shepherds were sitting by a big fire. They were staying awake to make sure that their sheep came to no harm.

The fire kept them warm, and the wild animals stayed well away from the flames.

As the shepherds sat by their fire, an angel came to them. "I have good news for you!" he said. "You must share it with all the men and women – and the children, too – who are God's friends.

"Tell them that the Baby Jesus has been born. He is Christ, your Lord! You will find him in Bethlehem, in a stable, lying in a manger."

Suddenly the sky was filled with light, and a great choir of angels began to sing,

> *"Glory be to God!*
> *And Peace to all*
> *who are God's friends!"*

After the angels had gone, the shepherds hurried away to Bethlehem and there they found the stable.

The shepherds tiptoed in and looked at the baby lying in his manger. They told Mary and Joseph what the angels had said about Jesus.

Mary listened in wonder. She understood that one day Jesus would do special work for God.

When the shepherds had said goodbye to Jesus, they went outside and whooped for joy!

On the way home they sang and shouted, telling everyone they met about the Baby Jesus. They thanked God for sending him to them.

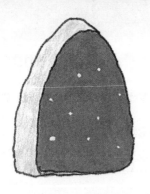

In a land far away to the East, three Wise Men had seen a bright new star in the sky.

Because of their great learning, they knew that it was the star of a newborn king.

The star began to move across the sky, and the Wise Men decided to follow it. They hoped that it would lead them to the Baby King.

The journey of the Wise Men was
long and difficult. Even their
camels grew tired.

But at last they reached Bethlehem.
And there the star came to rest
over the place where Jesus lay.

The Wise Men were full of joy as they hurried in to Jesus. When they saw him lying in his mother's arms they fell to their knees before him.

Each of them had brought a special gift for the newborn king.

One had brought gold, because Jesus was a king.

One had brought frankincense – a sweet-smelling incense – because it showed that it was God who had sent Jesus to Mary.

One had brought bitter myrrh, because one day Jesus would suffer and die.

When the Wise Men had given their gifts to Jesus, they began their long journey back to their homelands.

Mary and Joseph left Bethlehem, too. But instead of going straight home to Nazareth they took Baby Jesus to the great Temple in Jerusalem.

They did this to show that their son belonged to God.

At last, Mary and Joseph went home to Nazareth with their baby.

Jesus grew up wise and strong, a boy loved by God and by everyone who knew him.